The Essence of Spiritual Wisdom:

Beyond Religions

Presented in diagrams for easier understanding

by

Lord Tengku Seraski Koling Mochtar

Design: Lord Tengku Seraski Koling Mochtar.

Copyright © 2016 by Lord Tengku Seraski Koling Mochtar.

Published by Heavenly Ltd publishing.

ISBN-13: 978-1537293479

ISBN-10: 1537293478

Lord.Tengku.Mochtar@gmail.com

For my beloved family

The Essence of Spiritual Wisdom: Beyond Religions

Content

Definition: THE ONE

A "Name" is nothing other than a term used for identification.

In this book, to help our limited mind to understand better, we will use the term "THE ONE" to refer to The single, absolute, indivisible REALITY.

In truth:
- The name that can be named is not the eternal name. The name you can say isn't the real name.

- If you can talk about it, it ain't the REALITY. If it has a name, it's just another thing.

- The nameless is the origin of Heaven and Earth.

Names are used to differentiate things.

Does The ONE need a name when everything is The ONE Himself?

Names did not exist prior to creation of universes.

The nameless REALITY is the Source of universe.

Chapter 1

Everything is THE ONE,
the All-Loving, the Ever-Loving

There is nothing but THE ONE. Everything else does not exist.

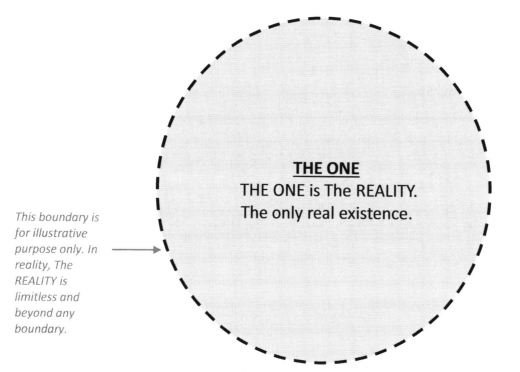

THE ONE
THE ONE is The REALITY.
The only real existence.

This boundary is for illustrative purpose only. In reality, The REALITY is limitless and beyond any boundary.

Nothingness
There is nothing but The REALITY. Everything else does not exist.

*"**THE ONE is Indivisible.**"*
(Indivisible = The reality/the inner essence of everything =
Indivisible Oneness)

THE ONE wants to experience His Majestic and Grand Self. So, He creates human.

To experience being...	Require...
The Merciful	→ The object of mercy
The Compassionate	→ The object of compassion
The Creator	→ The creation
The Powerful	→ The powerless
The Protector	→ The protected
The Forgiving	→ The forgiven
The Loving	→ The loved
The Holy	→ The unholy
The Patient	→ The object of patient

THE ONE wants to experience Himself. However, there is nothing but Him.

This is why human is created. So that THE ONE can bestow His limitless love. After all, He is the Merciful and the Compassionate.

This list is not exhaustive as The REALITY is limitless.

"I have created the spiritual beings and men only so that they may serve Me (by means of receiving the Love of THE ONE). I do not ask for provision from them; nor do I want them to feed Me."

Human is created limited on the outside but limitless in the inside.

Human is created limited on the outside because only the limited can appreciate the limitless.

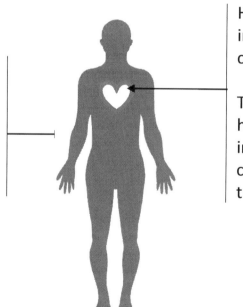

Human is created limitless in the inside because only the limitless can comprehend the limitless.

THE ONE bestows limitless into human by blowing part of His Soul into human. As the result, human contains a part of THE ONE within the deepest part of his soul-heart.

The position and shape of the soul-heart are for illustrative purpose only.
The soul-heart, unlike the physical heart which pumps the blood, is not physical.

*"**Then He proportioned him** (human's physical body) **and breathed into him from His Own Spirit** (human's soul is part of THE ONE's spirit)*. ***And He made for you hearing, sight and hearts*** *(perception, vision, and reflection are only possible due to the Spirit of THE ONE within human)**."***

The physical universes are created for the physical human to gain experiences within it.

By creating the universes, THE ONE creates polarity within Himself:

- Spiritual
- Limitless
- Hidden
- Creator
- Holy
- Eternal
- Independent

- Physical
- Limited
- Manifested
- Created
- Unholy
- Temporary
- Dependent

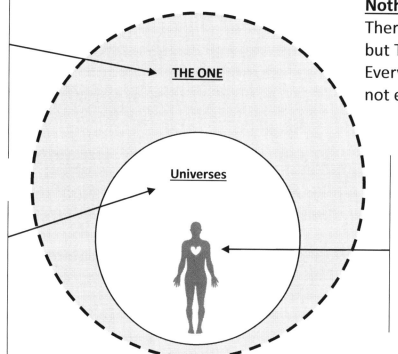

THE ONE

Universes

Nothingness
There is still nothing but The REALITY. Everything else does not exist.

Human
Being with the attributes of universe on the outside and the attributes of THE ONE in the inside.

"It is He who has spread out the earth for His creatures."

Through what human sees, feels, experiences, THE ONE experiences His Majestic Self.

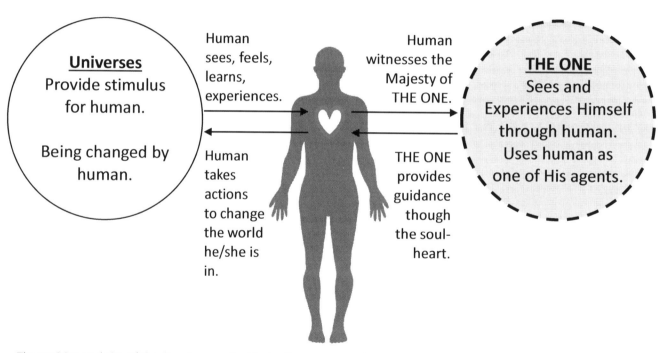

Universes
Provide stimulus for human.

Being changed by human.

Human sees, feels, learns, experiences.

Human takes actions to change the world he/she is in.

Human witnesses the Majesty of THE ONE.

THE ONE provides guidance though the soul-heart.

THE ONE
Sees and Experiences Himself through human. Uses human as one of His agents.

The position and size of the drawings are for illustrative purpose only.
In reality, everything is part of The REALITY.

"He is with you, wherever you may be. And THE ONE sees well all that ye do."

"I am his hearing with which he hears, his seeing with which he sees, his hands with which he strikes, and his foot with which he walks."

In sum, the true purpose of human life is to be, to experience, and to become a witness.

This is why human seeks and thrilled by experience because the true purpose of human is to be, to experience, and to witness the Majesty and the Grandness of THE ONE—whether manifested in the universes or hidden in the deepest places, whether he/she are aware or unaware of it.

The illustration is not exhaustive. Even the unhappy experience is an experience to be experienced.

"I am a Hidden Treasure,
and I long to be known,
so I create a creation,
to which I make Myself known,
so that they know Me."

"Behold! In the creation of the heavens and the earth...
there are indeed Signs for men of understanding."

Human has the potential to realise his/her true self and to become limitless.

THE ONE breathes part of His Soul into human so that human become limitless—as <u>only</u> the limitless can comprehend The Limitless. Without It, it will be impossible for human to comprehend The Limitless.

Once human realises this, he/she can experience this limitless as well. In other words, human has the potential to exhibit the attributes of THE ONE in the physical universes.

This is why human is also called the representative of THE ONE on the earth.

This list is not exhaustive as the attributes of The REALITY is limitless in nature.

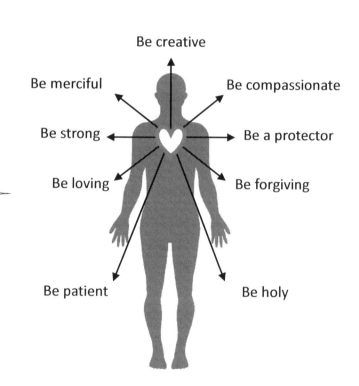

Be creative

Be merciful

Be compassionate

Be strong

Be a protector

Be loving

Be forgiving

Be patient

Be holy

"Consider the human self, and how it is formed in accordance with what it is meant to be. And how it is imbued with moral failings as well as with consciousness of THE ONE! To a happy state shall indeed attain he who causes this (potential) to grow in purity. And truly lost is he who buries it (squander his true potential).

Chapter 2

Praises be to THE ONE, the Shaper of worlds

When THE ONE creates the universes, it happens in three step process.

Thought	Word	Action
When THE ONE intends a thing...	...THE ONE says to it: "Be!"...	...and it is!
THE ONE wills for the heavens and the earth to be...	He says unto them "Be"	And the heavens and earth become exist
THE ONE plans for Mary to have son without being touched	He says to the plan "Be"	And Mary has Jesus
THE ONE wants to create Adam from dust	He says to dust "Be"	And Adam be
When THE ONE wants the Day of Judgment	He says "Be"	And His word comes true
Spiritual level	**Symbolic level**	**Physical level**

"When He wills a thing,
He only says to it 'Be' and it is."

You are a spiritual being which is contained in a physical vessel.

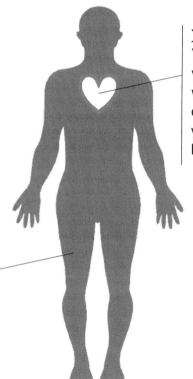

The real you
Your true self is your soul-heart, which is contained within your physical body.

Your avatar
Your physical body, while yours, is not the true you. It is just a temporary vehicle you use in this physical world.

Sometimes we mistakenly think that our physical body is us.

Human is not a physical being who experiences a spiritual journey.

Human is a spiritual being who experiences a physical journey.

"Neither My Earth nor My Heavens can contain Me, but the heart of a Believer, contains Me."

Because human represents The Limitless, human has the power of creation.

Thought	Word	Action
When human has an idea which he/she intends to make it comes true...	...he/she will elaborate the idea, explain it, and structure it...	...and he/she must take actions to make the plan comes true

For example:

- Idea
- Conception
- Visualisation
- Business idea
- Ideal house idea
- Aspiration to change the world

- Plan
- Presentation
- Model
- Business plan
- Architecture drawing
- Speech to convince people

- Action
- Achievement
- Real product
- Running business
- Built house
- Actions undertaken

Spiritual level

Symbolic level

Physical level

*"**If My creations ask you about Me** (tell them): **I am indeed very close** (within themselves). **I respond to the prayer** (the wish) **of every suppliant who call Me** (everyone who has a wish)."*

Your spiritual self has the power to change your physical reality.

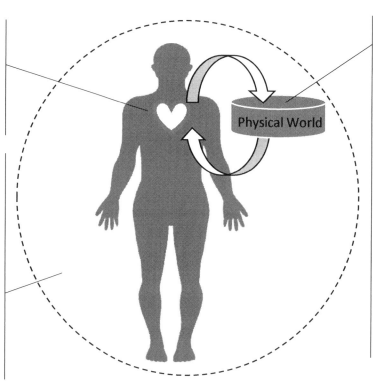

Spiritual self
Your physical body contains your soul-heart i.e. your spiritual self.

Spiritual reality
You are living in a giant spiritual ocean which permeates everything in the physical world. Your soul-heart can control this sea as they are closely connected.

Physical World

Physical reality
Your soul-heart sends out waves of energy. Its vibration will affect the spiritual ocean to bring into physical world what you think about. After all, the physical world is just a manifestation of the spiritual energy.

As the result, what you think of can become a physical reality. Just like the process of creation. Therefore, control your thoughts carefully.

"*I am as my creations thinks of me.*"

Be a positive thinker, so that you always attract positive things toward you!

Self-fulfilling prophecy: You are what you think.

If you think about positive things...	...you will send positive signals...	...and therefore attract positive things.

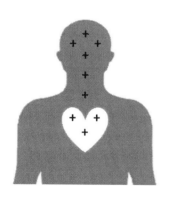 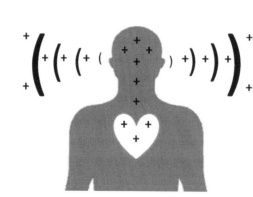 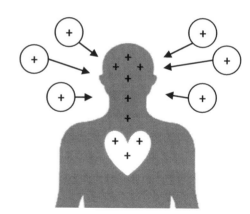

"Assume the best about THE ONE."

"If you are grateful,
I will surely add more (favours) unto you."

Human always creates, even when he/she does not aware of it or does not want it.

Therefore, watch over your thoughts. Negative thoughts manifest into negative reality. Positive thoughts manifest into positive reality. Most people sabotage themselves.

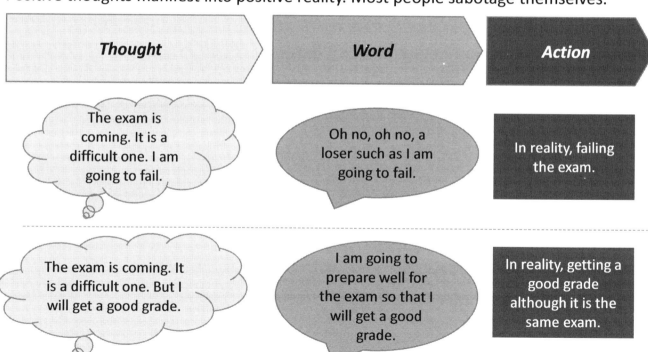

*"**Man prays for evil** (by thinking negatively) **just as he prays for good** (thinking positively)**; and Man is indeed hasty** (not careful of what he/she thinks)."*

Be careful of your thoughts, as you have the power to manifest them into the reality!

Self-fulfilling prophecy: You are what you think.

If you think about negative things...

...you will send negative signals...

...and therefore attract negative things.

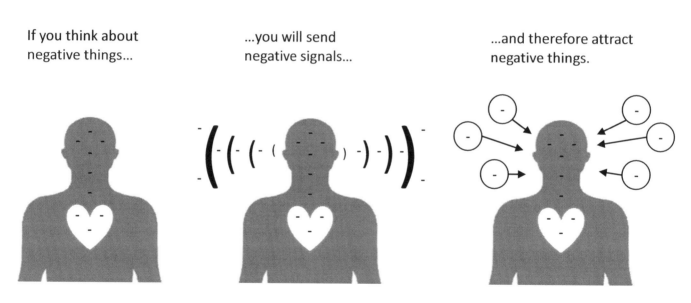

*"**Stirred to anxiety by their own feeling** (negative things in life are due to one's own thinking), **moved by wrong suspicions of THE ONE** (i.e. by thinking negatively about The Universes) – **suspicions due to ignorance** (while actually The REALITY is not negative).*"

Chapter 3

The All-Loving,
The Ever-Loving

THE ONE creates the rules of the systems but human has freedom to choose.

Your choice of action will determine whether you will improve yourself or not.

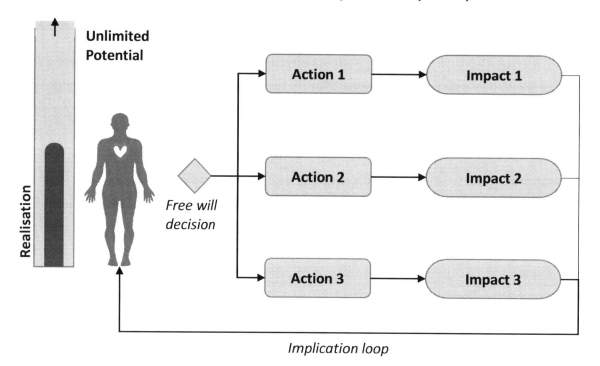

42

"Indeed, we offered the Trust (free will) to the heavens (the soul-heart) and the earth (the physical body) and the mountains (the organs), and they declined to bear it and feared it; but Man (the consciousness) undertook to bear it.

For human to have the full experience, THE ONE grants human with free choice and will.

Human can decide and determine their own fate:

Before coming to the physical world, while still in spiritual world, in the shape of a little soul

During the stay in the physical world, after coming from the spiritual world, in the shape of a human

I want to experience being...

e.g.
- A woman
- From Asia
- Born in a lower-class family
- Strong despite hardships/challenges
- etc

Some choices, made previously, is not alterable anymore in this world e.g. being a woman, born from a lower-class family in Asia. But most other choices are yours to make and alter:

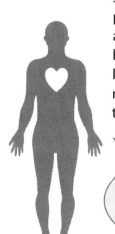

I choose to improve my life and become better despite my initial starting point

"No misfortune can happen on earth or in your souls but is recorded in a decree before We bring it into existence (we chose already for ourselves what events we want to experience before we came to this physical world, but how we react to the events is up to our free will)."

Since THE ONE has bestowed us with free choice, He will not intervene in our choices.

THE ONE will always guide you to the right choices as He wants you to be happy. However, He will not stop you from choosing the wrong choices as you are free to choose.

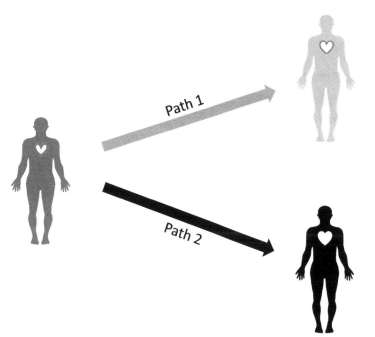

Whatever you choose, it is part of the experience you want to experience. The consequences are all yours. Blame no one else.

If you can shape your own experience, then why don't you choose the experiences that will make you happy? The experiences that make you happy are experiences which allow you to express your true self – the soul in you.

46

"Had THE ONE willed, they would not have taken gods."
(The REALITY will not intervene with our free will, even when we choose wrongly)

When a new soul is born into the physical world, he/she has first to forget everything.

This is because if human knows about his/her limitless from the beginning, he/she cannot fully experience being limited.

Before coming to the physical world, you know who you are	*During the stay in the physical world, you forget who you are and experience who you are not*	*A moment before leaving the physical world, you will see with clarity*

I know who I am. I know I am part of the Limitless. But I want to experience the beauty of being Limitless.

Who am I? Why I am here? Why there are so many limitations? If only there were no limits.

I remember again!

Some of us do remember who we truly are in this world and experience true joy and excitement

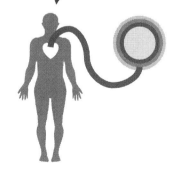

"(It will be said to the soul of the death) **Certainly you were heedless of it** *(you did not remember about it while in the world),* **but now We have removed from you your veil, so your sight today is sharp** *(after death, you remember again that you are actually part of The REALITY)."*

THE ONE only creates goodness. Evilness is nothing other than the absence of goodness.

Cold = the absence of heat.
The coldest temperature possible is 0° K when there is zero heat (calor). There is no maximum heat possible.

Dark = the absence of light.
The darkest condition possible is 0 Lm when there is zero light (lumen). There is no maximum brightness possible.

Evilness = the absence of Goodness.
The absolute evil is nothing other than when there is zero goodness. There is no maximum goodness possible.

Sadness = the absence of Happiness.
The absolute sadness is nothing other than when there is zero happiness. There is no maximum happiness possible.

Limited = the absence of Limitless.
The absolute limitation is when everything is limited. There is no limit to limitless.

THE ONE only creates the goodness.

Sadness exists so that human can appreciate happiness.

Evilness exists so that so that human can appreciate goodness.

Limitation exists so that human can appreciate limitless.

"My mercy encompasses everything
(everything is created from and for Mercy)."

The sufferings in this world are due to either human's collective or individual choices.

War, Economic crisis, Poverty, Climate change, Slavery, Crime, and any other sufferings are all caused by human choices – either collectively or individually.

Some people choose it. Some people simply do not care. Some people just do nothing about it. Not caring about it or not taking action on it is the same as choosing it.

There is no point in blaming THE ONE for our fate as we are the one who choose and create our own fate. We have already been given a power of creation and a gift of free will to change the world we live in. This is why: surely THE ONE does not change the condition of a people until they change their own condition – either by their hands or by their hearts.

"I have forbidden oppression for myself…"

Since all of us is a manifestation of THE ONE, we inherently have the power to change our world.

Everybody wants to live in a better world.

Some of us do nothing about it.

Everybody has capacity to make world a better place.

Some of us pretend not having it.

Some of us choose to neglect it.

Some of us choose ignore it.

But the power is always there inside us.

"...those who, when an oppressive wrong is inflicted on them, (are not cowed but) help and defend themselves."

Chapter 4

The Revealer at the revelation day

THE ONE is full of love. He is not crazy for worship nor seeking to torture us.

The Characteristics of THE ONE		Implication
The Self Sufficient	THE ONE does not need your worship. He is not a power hungry dictator.	No one is going to be punished by not worshipping THE ONE. He sends guidance to us because THE ONE wants happiness for us.
The Merciful	THE ONE is not looking to torture you. He is not a blood thirsty tyrant. After all what is the point of torturing people when you give them free choice?	No one is going to be burned alive for eternity due to not worshipping THE ONE. Hell is nothing after than disappointment of not meeting your true potential. THE ONE sends warning to us because He does not want us to be disappointed later in the future.
The Loving-Kindness	THE ONE wants happiness for us. He is like a loving parent.	THE ONE is full of love. He wants us to be happy, enjoy ourselves, and experience this world to the fullest. So, live your life to the fullest.

"My Mercy prevails over My Wrath..."

"Do you think a woman will ever throw her child in the fire? No. THE ONE is even more merciful to His creations than a woman is to her child!"

Death is basically a process of returning into THE ONE and rejoining Him.

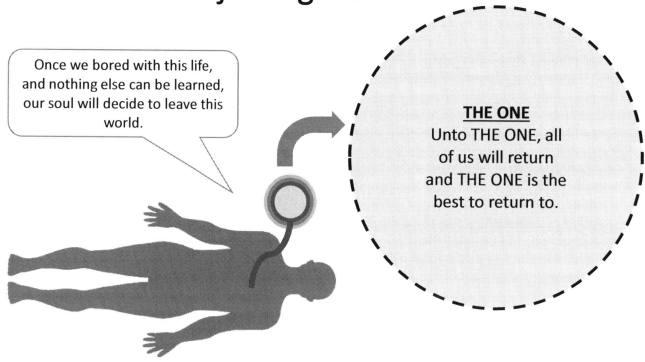

Once we bored with this life, and nothing else can be learned, our soul will decide to leave this world.

THE ONE
Unto THE ONE, all of us will return and THE ONE is the best to return to.

Death is made mandatory because THE ONE loves each of us and does not want to miss us.

60

"To THE ONE we belong (part of The REALITY), to Him we shall return (rejoining Him)."

"Everyone on the earth is transitory. But the Face of Your Creator (the absolute reality of the essence of human) will live forever—full of Majesty, Bounty and Honour. Which, then, of the favours of Your Creator will you deny?"

Heaven is the great joy of returning to THE ONE and becoming limitless once again.

A paradise would be meaningless if we do not return to THE ONE.

Heaven is not a place, it is a state of mind.

Heaven is nothing other than the realisation of all the good things we have done to other people (which are also ourselves), the satisfaction of living up to our true potential, and the joy of becoming Limitless again after experiencing limitation.

This diagram is for illustrative purpose only. Heaven is not a physical object.

*"**For them there will be Paradises** (i.e. the plane of perfect consciousness) **beneath which rivers** (symbol of the endless Mercy of THE ONE) **flow.**"*

Hell is the great disappointment of not living up to one's own true potential.

There is no hell. Why does the Merciful THE ONE want to torture and burn the soul? After all, everything is the manifestation of Himself.

Hell is not a place. It is a state of mind.

Hell is nothing other than the realisation of all the bad things we have done to other people (which are also ourselves), and the disappointment of not living up to our true potential.

This diagram is for illustrative purpose only. Hell is not a physical object.

"I do call to witness the revelation day, and I do call to witness the self-reproaching soul (when the real truth being revealed, the soul will realise all of his/her errs)."

"Fear the fire (spiritual anguish), whose fuel is men and stones (driven by blindly following others and over attachment to material objects)."

Angels and Satans are within yourself. You are the one in control of your body.

Within human's soul-heart		
Angels...	**Adam...**	**Satans...**
...are the true potential of the man, which represent the attributes of THE ONE:	...is the conscious mind which control the body, make choices, and exercise free will:	...are the man's basic instincts which are designed to preserve man in the physical world:
• Creative • Merciful • Compassionate • Strong • Protective • Forgiving • Loving • Patient • Kind • etc	• Reason • Intelligence • Conscience • etc The command centre / ruler which must decide which direction he/she wants to go to.	• Pride • Greed • Envy • Lust • Backbiting • Stinginess • Malice • etc

"**Your Creator said to the angels** *(personification of your soul-heart)*: '***I will make upon the earth*** *(your physical body)* ***a vicegerent*** *(your conscious mind).'* "

"*(Satan i.e. personification of bodily instincts)* **said: "I am better than him** *(instincts do not want to be controlled by the conscious mind).* **You created me from fire** *(passion).'* "

Basic instincts are nothing other than mechanism to protect and enhance life.

Instinct	Incentive for	Purpose
Lust	Human to reproduce	Bring another soul to the physical earth to witness the Grandness and Majesty of THE ONE
Fear	Human to avoid dangers	Avoid things that could cause harms and prematurely cut short human's experience in this physical world
Greed	Human to collect good things for them	For basic survival, comfort and future opportunities
Pride	Human to accomplish great things	So that human wants to do great things and achieve greatness

*"**He** (Satan, your instincts) **swore to them** (i.e. Adam, your conscious mind, and Eve, your subconscious mind)**, 'Indeed, I am from among the advisors'.** (instinct aims to protect the physical body) "*

*"**Whoever deserts THE ONE and takes Satan as master** (following bodily temptations instead of higher consciousness) **has certainly suffered a great loss** (fail to see true self)."*

Once one realises who he/she is, he/she will wish to return to THE ONE.

A little soul, once it realises that it is not its physical body but part of something much grander and majestic, will want to...

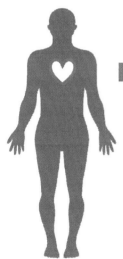

...to return to the Grand and Majestic Source, to become one with the Source.

If its time not yet come, it will seek to witness more the Grandness and Majesty of THE ONE.

THE ONE
Unto THE ONE, all of us will return.

"O, peaceful soul (a soul which has satisfied in experiencing the physical reality)**, return to your Creator** (the Source of your true essence) **well-pleased and well-pleasing** (due to successfully experiencing Limitation). **Enter, then, among my creations** (rejoining other souls who have returned to the Source) **and enter my Paradise** (rejoining THE ONE)

Chapter 5

All is for You, All is from You

There is no great God in the distant space who sends commands via His winged angels.

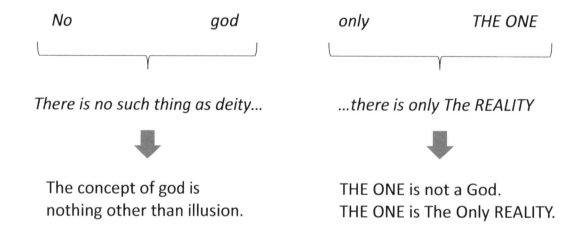

No   god   only   THE ONE

There is no such thing as deity...   *...there is only The REALITY*

The concept of god is
nothing other than illusion.

THE ONE is not a God.
THE ONE is The Only REALITY.

Don't imagine there is a great God in the distant space who sends commands via His winged angels to His prophets on earth!

"...There is no god, only HE..."
(HE = The inner essence/the Reality of everything)

One's fate is one's own responsibilities as there is no God that oppresses and punishes.

You are the one who is responsible for your thoughts, actions, and fate. THE ONE has granted you with everything you need. So, do not waste your life and start experience greatness.

"Let him who finds good, praise THE ONE and let him who finds other than that blame no one but himself."

You, others, and everything in this world are essentially the same.

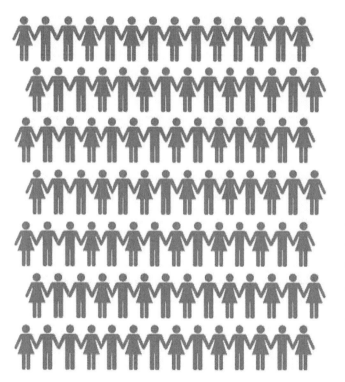

Since THE ONE is the only reality and there is nothing else but THE ONE, everything and every person is a manifestation of THE ONE (be careful: this does not mean everyone is THE ONE, the Absolute REALITY).

If you are a manifestation of THE ONE and others are also manifestation of THE ONE, then others are essentially you.

What goodness you do to others is goodness you do to yourself and THE ONE. What badness you do to others is badness you do to yourself and THE ONE.

You = Others = Everything in this world = the Essence of THE ONE.

"You are all from each other."

Therefore, treat others as you would like to be treated.

Verily, on the Day of Revelation, THE ONE will ask His creations:

- **THE ONE:** O, human, I asked you for food but you did not feed me.
- **Human:** How could I feed you? You are the Lord of the worlds!
- **THE ONE:** Did you not know that my creation felt hunger, and you did not feed him. Alas, had you fed him you would have found Me with him.

- **THE ONE:** O, human, I was thirsty but you gave Me nothing to drink.
- **Human:** How could I give You drink? You are the Lord of the worlds!
- **THE ONE:** Did you not know that my creation felt thirsty and you did not give him drink. Alas, if you had given him, you would have found Me with him.

- **THE ONE:** O, human, I was sick and you did not visit Me.
- **Human:** How can I visit You? You are the Lord of the worlds!
- **THE ONE:** Did you not know that my creation was sick and you did not visit him. Alas, had you visited him, you would have found Me with him.

"Do good to you parents, relatives, orphans, the needy, close neighbours and far neighbours, your fellow travellers, those who are stranded, and those under your hand."

THE ONE is constantly communicating to human, to help us realise our true potential.

THE ONE uses many medium to communicate with human.

It could be through sudden inspiration, dream, sound of winds, neighbour's chatters, lyrics in the latest pop music, fallen leaves, someone else's advice, etc.

But not many people are listening. Most people ignore the messages because they don't believe that THE ONE wants to communicate with them.

"It is not fitting for a man that THE ONE should speak to him (because words are limited and cannot convey the exact meaning perfectly and THE ONE is Limitless) except by inspiration (which can convey the exact message unlike words), or from behind a veil (indirect method if inspiration fails), or by the sending of a messenger (if indirect methods fails)..."

THE ONE also send prophets so that human can hear directly from another human being.

Prophets are sent to relay the messages and teach the ultimate truth to others. So that it is easier for human to understand the messages.

But in the end, there is no compulsion of following the messages. Human are free to choose whether they want to follow or not.

"We sent Prophets as bringers of glad tidings and as warners..."

"There is no compulsion in religion. Verily, Truth stands out clearly from Error."

Saint is a human who has realised who he/she is and what his/her true potential is.

Once a person realises his/her true nature, he/she becomes a saint. Saints are the ones who have attained enlightenment.

Sainthood is different than prophethood because saints are not directly tasked by THE ONE to spread their understanding. Nonetheless, saints usually go to teach and help others to realise their true potentials.

The line of prophethood have ceased, but the line of sainthood have not ceased.

The pictures presented here are illustrative. We do not have the complete list of prophets nor saints.

"We have sent you inspiration, as We sent it to Noah and the Messengers after him. We sent inspiration to Abraham, Ishmael, Isaac, Jacob, and the Tribes, to Jesus, Job, Jonah, Aaron, and Solomon, and to David We gave the Psalms."

Chapter 6

Show us the rising path

Human attains true happiness by manifesting his/her potential i.e. the traits of THE ONE.

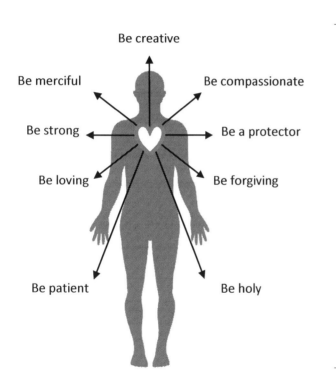

Be creative

Be merciful

Be compassionate

Be strong

Be a protector

Be loving

Be forgiving

Be patient

Be holy

Attain true happiness by being the highest and best version of who you can be.

Experience greatness and grandness.

Show others the majesty of yourself (and hence of THE ONE's)

For illustrative purpose only. Not an exhaustive list of the names of THE ONE.

"Without doubt, in the remembrance of THE ONE (by experiencing/manifesting the beautiful characteristics of THE ONE) do soul-hearts find satisfaction (be happy).

Prophets and Saints are people who have attained understanding of the real truth.

Prophets are men who are instructed by THE ONE to teach the others. Saints are people who have attained understanding of the real truth. They are not instructed to teach the others, but usually they choose to do so. One doesn't need special education, special training, or special title, etc, to become a saint/prophet. Even a poor and illiterate man can be a saint/prophet.

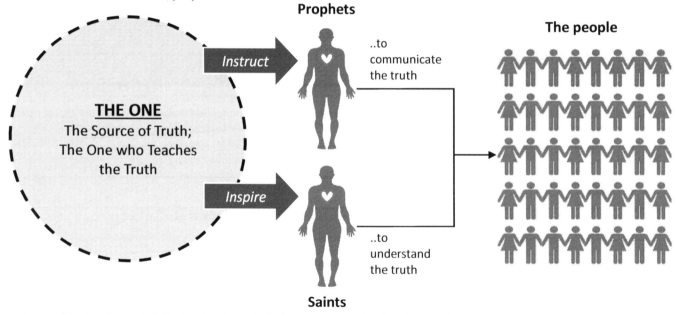

The smaller size of people is for illustration only, it does not mean that Prophets and Saints are more important than anyone.

"We assuredly sent amongst every community a messenger (to teach) serve THE ONE (manifesting the good characteristics of The REALITY) and eschew evil."

"...We make no distinction between one and another of His Messengers..."

Religions and rituals are mechanisms men devised to realise ones' own potential.

Worship rituals are nothing other than mechanisms that men devised to realise ones' own potential. A mechanism may or may not work for you. Therefore, You don't have to follow any ritual which does not work for you. You should find/choose/create a mechanism which works for you i.e. a worship ritual which allows you to realise your true self.

All worship rituals here are for illustration only.
The author does not condemn nor promote any particular religion.

"For you is your religion and for me is my religion!"

Wisdom #39

Holy books can only guide us if we are prepared to discern their hidden meanings.

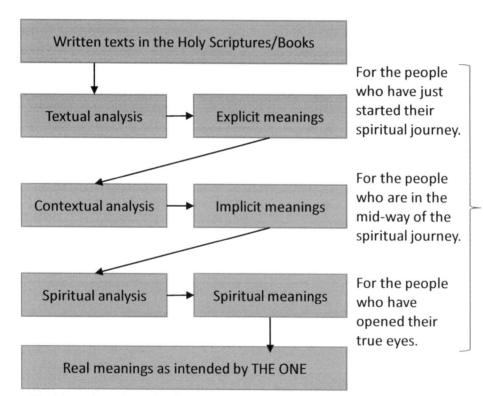

Written texts in the Holy Scriptures/Books	
Textual analysis → Explicit meanings	For the people who have just started their spiritual journey.
Contextual analysis → Implicit meanings	For the people who are in the mid-way of the spiritual journey.
Spiritual analysis → Spiritual meanings	For the people who have opened their true eyes.
Real meanings as intended by THE ONE	

Holy Books are designed to suit different levels of understanding.

The literal texts are for the novices of spiritual journey. But, for the adepts, there are hidden meanings behind hidden meanings behind the texts.

Deeper spiritual insights can only be understood by people who ponder on the real meanings of the texts. Unfortunately, most people do not analyse the meanings behind the texts.

The hierarchy is shown for illustrative purpose only. In reality, understanding is a continuous spectrum.

"And verily, We have coined for mankind in the Holy Book every kinds of similitudes, so that they may reflect."

"Indeed, the worst of living creatures in the sight of THE ONE are the deaf (do not hear reasons) *and dumb* (do not use their soul-heart to think), *who do not use their reason* (do not analyse)

Wisdom #40

In analysing the Holy Books, one must always listen to his/her soul-heart.

How can we arrive at the correct understanding of the real meanings of the Holy Books' texts?

How can one ensure the textual, contextual or spiritual analysis is correct?

The answer is simple. Let your grandest, deepest, purest feelings i.e. your soul-heart to guide you.

You can never go wrong by following your soul-heart. And when it comes from your soul-heart, you will know for sure.

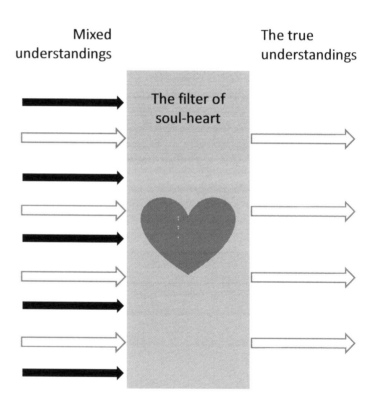

Mixed understandings — The filter of soul-heart — The true understandings

*"...He inspired it (the soul) **what is wrong for it and what is right for it.**"*

Prayers are basically a technique to focus the creative power within you.

THE ONE has granted us the power to create what we want with our own power. And prayer is nothing other than a technique to concentrate and use the creative power within you to get what you want.

By willing/wanting something, then uttering it in prayers, you actually move it from *thought* realm to *word* realm.

By really believing that your prayers will be granted, you are actually sending instruction with strong emotional/ spiritual power for it to be realised.

Your instruction then will be received by the Universe to be realised as long as it does not conflict with the rules of the system.

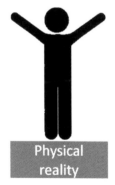

Physical reality

In summary, you have the power to change the physical reality via your own mind. Prayer is a technique to help you do that. The speed of realisation is depending on how strong your will and conviction are. If nothing happens, then pray more with a stronger belief!

Agent(s) of The REALITY will then bring what you want/will into the physical reality. The agent(s) can be other people or even you, yourself.

"Who is calling upon me that I may answer him? Who is asking from me that I may give him? Who is seeking my forgiveness that I may forgive him?"

Three secrets of a granted prayer.

(1) You really want it.
You are very clear of what you want. You know vividly and in details what you want and why you want it. You can imagine the feeling when you have it. And you know with certainty that it is really, really good for you.

(2) You strongly believe that THE ONE will give it to you.
You are really sure that it will be given to you because it is good for you as well as for others. In fact, you already know that it has been given to you and it is actually coming toward you. Therefore, you praise THE ONE and send your best gratitude to Him. There is nothing for you to worry about.

(3) It does not against the rules of the system
What you ask does not violate the rules of the system. For example, you cannot breathe in water. You cannot live forever. You cannot fly without using a device. You cannot change your past. But you can change almost everything else.

The key to a granted prayer is focus and persistence. The more you want it, the more you focus on it, the more you will get it.

And don't doubt that you won't get it because The Universe responds to your mind. If you think so, it will be so. When you doubt, you will think of not getting it and therefore becoming really not getting it. So, doubt not and have faith.

*"**When you beseech THE ONE in supplication** (when you want something from The REALITY)**, be convinced that He will answer you.** (be convinced that it will come true)"*

Chapter 7

The path of the enlightened ones

Everyone has the same destination, but each one of us can take different paths.

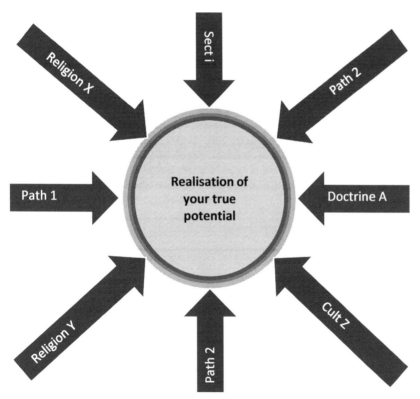

The actions, rituals, ceremonies, symbols, sacred objects, artefacts, etc may be different. But as long as the path is heading toward the Source, they are all the same.

There are many paths to THE ONE. Some paths are better than the others. But please do not think other people are doomed just because they are not in the same path as of yours. As long as they have the same destination, i.e. toward the Source, which paths they take are irrelevant.

Please do not follow a path blindly. Don't be trapped in a dogma. Check if the destination is the one you want to head to. Check if the path is suitable with your soul-heart. Always follow your soul-heart in your journey.

"And every one has a direction to which he should turn (own path to take), *therefore hasten to good works* (realise your potential); *wherever you are, THE ONE will bring you all together* (you will rejoin THE ONE); *surely THE ONE has power over all things.*

"A man said: THE ONE will not forgive this person! THE ONE the Exalted said: Who is he who swore by me that I will not forgive someone? I have forgiven him..."

The strayed ones are no other than people who ignore their true potential.

Prophets have come again and again to teach people the same thing i.e. the real truth, for example:

	Key Lesson		Key Lesson
Noah	If you are not controlling your mind, you will be drowned in the flood of ignorance. Controlling your mind will allow you to achieve higher state.	Moses	You are a god just because you have the power of creation. In the end, you are just a part of a whole.
Abraham	There is no point in worshiping external deities if the True REALITY is within your very self.	Jesus	Your thoughts and believes can change your reality. Once your ignorance is dead, your mind will resurrect into the higher consciousness.
Lot	Do not pursue only carnal desires as the true you is not your physical body.	Muhammad	There is no such thing as deities. There is only THE ONE, the REALITY. Everything else does not exist.

"O my creations who have transgressed against themselves (who have squandered their lives in pursuit of bodily pleasures), do not lose hope from the Mercy of THE ONE!"

Once you realise your true self, you should not disgrace your soul by worshiping objects.

You, yourself, is a manifestation of THE ONE. Why will you lower yourself? No matter how sacred an object is, nothing is more sacred than your very own soul. No point of worshipping objects.

Hallowed Statues

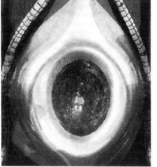
Magic Stones

Sacred Buildings

Holy Animals

Celestial Objects

Forms of Energy

Dead Saints

Living Saints

"Let not one of you belittle himself."

Prophets/saints can summon miracles as they know imagination has potential to be reality.

The saints who have understand the true nature of this universe can summon miracles...

...because they know imagination can be real if they will it.

Thought	Word	Action
• Imagination • Aspiration • Will	• Praying • Statement of will • Asking	Become a reality either by their own actions or other agents of universes.

Ones with strong will/faith/ believe can perform a miracle!

Examples of a miracle:

Split a sea

Heal sick people

Walk on water

"But one who had an understanding of the knowledge of the reality (a saint) said, 'I will bring it to you before you blink your eye (exercising a miracle of teleportation).' When Solomon saw the throne placed before him, he said: 'This (miracle) is by Mercy of my Creator... To see whether I will be grateful or ungrateful...' "

The power of creation does not belong to the Holy People only. Everyone has it.

Everyone of us is a creator. Everyone of us is creative. Everyone can become THE ONE's medium to create something new in this world. The creativity flows from our soul-heart.

No matter who you are, where you come from, what your background is, whether you are a good person or an evil person, you are always a creative being. Some of us may not realise it yet but every one of us is, in truth, a creator.

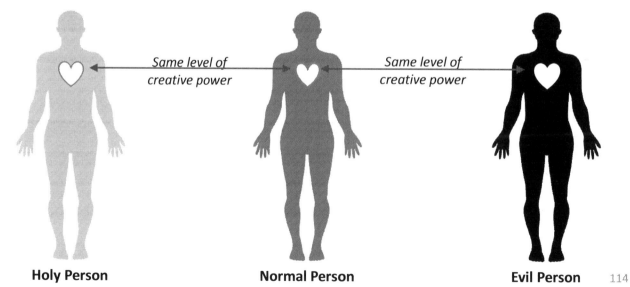

Holy Person   **Normal Person**   **Evil Person**   114

Same level of creative power

Same level of creative power

"O my creations, were the first of you and the last of you, the human of you and the spiritual being of you, to rise up in one place and make a request of me, and were I to give everyone what he requested, that would not decrease what I have any more than a needle would decrease the sea if put into it."

However, it does not mean you are The Absolute REALITY.

Human is manifestation of THE ONE, but is not THE ONE Himself. Don't be mistaken.

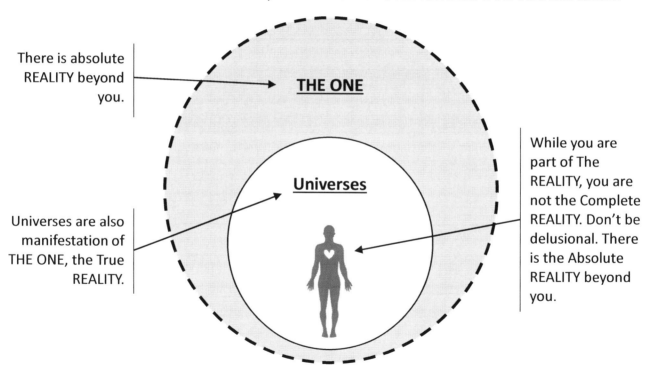

There is absolute REALITY beyond you.

THE ONE

Universes

Universes are also manifestation of THE ONE, the True REALITY.

While you are part of The REALITY, you are not the Complete REALITY. Don't be delusional. There is the Absolute REALITY beyond you.

"There is none like unto Him!
He sees and hears all."

All creative inspirations come from THE ONE, the Source. Human only serves as a medium.

All creative inspirations actually comes from THE ONE. Our power of creation is nothing other one of the many channels of THE ONE. In other word, we are only a medium of creation. When we create, THE ONE creates.

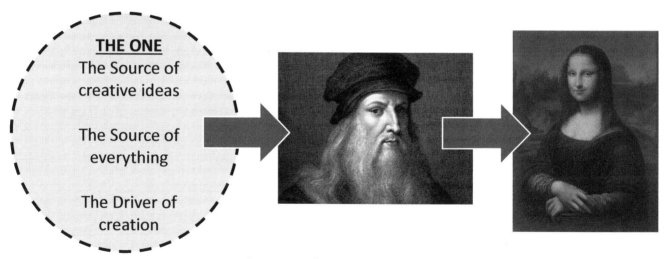

THE ONE
The Source of creative ideas

The Source of everything

The Driver of creation

The portrait of Mona Lisa and Leonardo Da Vinci are for illustrative purpose only. In reality, creative inspirations are not limited to the field of art.

"That is THE ONE, your Creator. There is no deities only He, the Creator of Everything. Therefore, serve Him (by being the medium of creation)*. He is the Bestower of Everything* (allow you to create with His power of creation)*."*

Epilogue

Let it be, O, Essence of universes

In the end, there is nothing but THE ONE. Everything else does not exist.

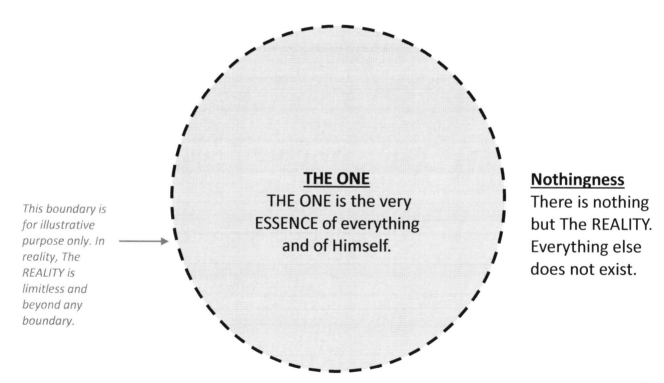

THE ONE
THE ONE is the very
ESSENCE of everything
and of Himself.

This boundary is for illustrative purpose only. In reality, The REALITY is limitless and beyond any boundary.

Nothingness
There is nothing but The REALITY. Everything else does not exist.

"At every instance He manifests Himself in yet another way!

"For THE ONE is All-Pervading..."

Closing words

All goods is from THE ONE and

He is the sole Guide along the Way.

All mistakes are mine and

THE ONE knows best.

Message from the author

Dear Reader,

Thank you very much for reading this book! I hope you find it helpful.

If you find this book helpful, I would appreciate it if you could help others to find this book too by:

- **Recommending it**. Please help other readers find this book by recommending it to friends, readers' groups, and discussion forums.

- **Reviewing it**. Please tell other readers what you liked or didn't like about this book by reviewing it at one of the major retailers, review sites, or your blog.

I really appreciate your kind help. May you find your path and realise your true potential.

Until next time,

Lord Tengku Seraski Koling Mochtar

About the author

Lord Tengku Seraski Koling Mochtar lives in Boston, USA. He spends his time trying to understand the secrets of creation and universes.

Credits

Cover, © Blue Sky, Createspace collection.

Wisdom 6, 20, 21, 24, 25, 33, 34, 38, 45, 48, © Various vector cliparts purchased from Shutterstock, Dreamstime, Canstockphoto, Gograph, or Getty Images. Pictures of a Golden Calf statue, Hajar Aswad, Kabah, Holy Cow, Moon, Fire, a Tomb of a saint, and a famous cleric. Names of the photographers are unknown.

Wisdom 30, The Creation of Adam, fresco painting by Michelangelo.

Wisdom 35, The portrait of Buddha, Lao Tzu, and Ibnu Al Arabi.

Wisdom 49, Self Portrait of Leonardo by Leonardo Da Vinci; Portrait of Mona Lisa by Leonardo Da Vinci.

Wisdom 1-49, Selected Texts from various sources.

Made in the USA
San Bernardino, CA
13 December 2016